INTUITION BREAKTHROUGH!

RECLAIM YOUR POWER
IN JUST A FEW MINUTES A DAY

TRISH MCKINNLEY

DAYTON, OH

7th STAR
PUBLISHING

Trish Mckinnley/7th Star Publishing
251 W. Central Ave, Suite 140,
Springboro, OH/USA 45458-6057

Ordering Information:
Quantity sales. Special discounts are available on quantity purchases by corporations, associations, and others. For details, contact the "Special Sales Department" at the address above.

Intuition Breakthrough/ Trish Mckinnley. —1st ed.

ISBN 9781733301589

CONTENTS

SECTION 1

SECTION 2

To my amazing children for your incredible love, trust and patience in being raised by a psychic mom.

To my beautiful stepdaughters for your openness to these gifts.

To my incredible husband, Jim, for celebrating the power of intuition and magic of love. Thank you for this dream come true!

To you, dear reader, for your intuition is a gift to the world. Thank you for entrusting me on your magical journey!

SECTION
01

WELCOME TO INTUITION BREAKTHROUGH...

Intuition. You already have it. But sometimes it's just so difficult to trust it.

Especially when so many people don't understand it!

Family, friends, and co-workers might think you sound crazy, and even worse, your own logic might be arguing against it!

But it's in you. And you know it. Because when you do trust your intuition, that's when you get the life you desire.

That's when you experience the peace and ease knowing you're making the right decision every single time.

No more "I should've listened."

In just a few minutes a day, let *Intuition Breakthrough* catapult your intuition to another dimension.

And once you break through, there's just no going back. Why would you want to?

Imagine the confidence you'll gain by recognizing and trusting your intuition.

Sometimes it doesn't make sense. You can't justify your reasoning. That gut feeling is often hard to explain to someone else.

But trusting your intuition is what will open the door to your new life. The one that is more peaceful and just plain easier!

It's time. Say goodbye to stress and worry. Say goodbye to second-guessing yourself. Say goodbye to regrets.

Say hello to *Intuition Breakthrough*.

You are in the right place!

First of all, this is the book you want to read if you have ever thought about things like...

That was meant to be.

Everything happens for a reason.

I knew that was going to happen.

Why didn't I listen to my feelings?

Or when you have witnessed the magic, but your rational thinking took over and told you it was just a coincidence, and just couldn't quite believe what just happened, actually happened.

I want to help you to see that the magic is real, and you can hear it if you tune and listen.

Hello Beautiful!

I'm Trish Mckinnley! I'm a lifetime psychic and creator of The Forgotten Tools of the Universe™ and Goddessology®. All the magical courses, workshops, videos, cheatsheets and daily manifesting exercises I've created and taught emerge from the lifetime foundation of working in this magical world.

I was raised as an out-of-the-closet intuitive.

My family looked normal. I *thought* we were normal. Sure, it might have been unique being raised in a multi-generational home, but I thought every family knew about angel communication, working with crystals, reading tarot cards and knowing which power animal to engage when you wanted something. And I DEFINITELY thought everyone knew their intuition was their unique super power.

Come to find out...*nope.*

Your natural gift - *your intuition* - has been downgraded to mute status.

And you're not alone! As an international psychic, my clients from all around the world - from Australia, to Japan to the UK, Canada, and US are saying the same thing.

Well, no more!

Your super Sixth Sense power needs to be heard! (And trusted! And have you confidently taking action). That is what led you to holding this book!

And, that's why I'm so passionate about teaching you how to strengthen your intuition.

To trust your intuitive voice.

And, to take action on your extra sensory powers – ESP - intuition.

I've taught thousands how to clear away the intuitive cobwebs and build that muscle so they have Olympic-sized intuition.... The kind that dazzles like the gold ring and achieves the happily-ever-after. Because baby, if you're happy then I'm happy! (And it raises the whole vibe of the world and the universe and the galaxy...)

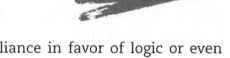

You do need to respect your unique super power of intuition.

It's going to take some work. (Of course it is! Think how long you've been ignoring or silencing your brilliance in favor of logic or even worrying what someone else will think. I get it.)

Each exercise is easy-to-do. But, you do have to do the task of observing, recognizing, and working your intuitive muscle.

You do need to believe in your knowingness.

And you do need to respect your unique super power of intuition.

About YOU...

You have a wonderful and accurate intuitive voice!

I know you've noticed your inner subtle nudges — you know, the messages that pop up and make you pause or say hmm.

Think about the times

- You suddenly saw a cardinal knowing it was your relative who had passed.

- You noticed the same numbers over and over and felt it meant something.

- Everything looked okay but you just sensed something was "off."

Yep. Your intuition was rocking out the communication.

You *know* your intuitive super power is within you.

However, with logic demanding attention, friends teasing you or family challenging you — it can be really a struggle to let your voice be heard.

These daily exercises bring crystal clear clarity to your intuitive voice. No more intuitive voice on "mute." These quick exercises create the habit of *hearing* and *trusting* your intuition.

You've heard "timing is everything."

You have to be at the right place, at the right time.

And you are!

You are already intuitively connecting!

Understanding Why This Works

"Everything is energy," said Albert Einstein. Including us. We're all dialed into energy. Energy is everywhere and in everything. We get to choose our level of connection.

We dial in for a stronger and louder signal through our physical senses. You intuitively receive messages through your five senses.

Your sight, often referred to as **Clairvoyance,** will provide intuitive messages as pictures, movies, or images that pop into your mind's eye. You'll spot an animal, color or number that seems random or out of place. Visual learners tend to excel using this sense.

Your hearing, often referred to as **Clairaudient,** is literally hearing messages in your head or hearing something off in a conversation, like when someone plays a wrong musical note. You'll pick up messages in song lyrics and mother nature chatter. Audio learners excel with this sense.

Your sense of smell, often referred to as **Clairalience,** is when you notice a scent like tobacco smoke or flowers, your dad's cologne or grandma's chocolate chip cookies and yet no one is there. You understand the term, "something doesn't smell right" and are often able to detect the subtle unique aromas in dishes and wine. A party for your nose!

Your taste, often referred to as **Clairgustance,** is when you notice a random flavor in your mouth like something sweet or spicy. As my grandma got older she couldn't taste her food, yet she could get a taste when receiving intuitive messages. How suhweet is that?!

Your sense of touch, often referred to as **Clairtangency,** is receiving the message through your hands. You can hold an antique ring in your hand and sense random details or lingering energy. This also provides insight when you touch someone. You'll just know things about them. Your hugs are often complimented!

And then there are those intuitive messages we get that are outside of the fabulous five senses called your sixth sense. There are two parts to your sixth sense, knowing and feeling.

Your sense of knowing, often referred to as **Claircognizant.** This is that gut instinct. You can't explain, it's a quick and immediate knowingness of information. You're not sure how it got there, but it's super relevant, important and right! This is also that instinct that saves your life.

Your sense of feeling, is often also referred to as **Clairsentient.** Feeling is your body giving you a tangible intuition reaction. You'll physically sense a yes or no answer. You'll experience a physical response like butterflies in your tummy or goose bumps on your arms. You are able to actually sense another's physical pain like a headache, healing from a sprain, or even heartache. On the brightside, you're also able to sense the physical joy of celebration and the euphoria of love. This sense also connects with the lingering energy in a room so you totally get the sentence, "the air was so thick you could cut it with a knife." This is great for the person saying they need a physical sign or confirmation of the intuitive message.

Listening. Really listening and trusting.

When you're going through day-to-day, you're being bombarded with messages. Observations of all types of data are flooding in. Sensory overload! However, your intuition is able to sort through the mounds of information quickly and accurately. You'll know that you know when you pause, dial into your intuition and trust the communication.

> *I'm here to help you determine and KNOW what your intuition is truly saying.*

I'm here to help you determine and KNOW what your intuition is truly saying. You must be ready too, or you wouldn't be here reading this! And I'm hoping you're excited to learn, because remember — intuition is a special ability, but it's also everybody's ability!

So many of us are beginning to tune into other ways of being. This is simply because, at long last, we are overriding our conditioning and listening to our soul's sweet magic.

Are you ready? Then let's begin!

Tuning Into YOU

This book is designed to be totally interactive. Each exercise will build on your natural intuitive abilities. You are super psychic. Your intuitive voice may be rather difficult to hear at the moment, but you will be hearing loud and clear by the end of this book. Yay!

I have included this quiz so you can figure out where you are in your Intuition Journey – and who doesn't love a fun quiz, right?

20 QUICK QUESTIONS TO DISCOVER YOUR STARTING POINT

Please, go through the quiz marking the first answer that pops into your mind. Don't overthink. Just trust your first response. Then at the end, tally the scores.

1. When you walk into a room, can you pick up the general "feel" of the place? Like "The air is so thick you can cut it with a knife." Or "Wow! This room feels warm and inviting!"

　　a) Nothing gets by me. I tap into my surroundings all the time.
　　b) I like to tune that stuff out.
　　c) Sometimes, maybe an afterthought? Sort of?

2. Do you have a built-in caller-ID?

　　a) I always know who is texting, calling or thinking of me!
　　b) Nope. I don't really care.
　　c) Sort of, I think so, now that you mention it.

3. Is there a go-to yummy treat that you turn to when you feel things are going miserably?

　　a) You bet! I love me some _____for those times.
　　b) No. I like my food to be an experience separate from anything I'm going through.
　　c) Chocolate. Donuts. Chips. I like it all, all the time, but I do grab even more when feeling stressed or upset.

4. What usually happens when you meet someone new?

a) Can't hide from me! I always know if they're a good thing or if I need to stay away from that character.
b) I don't care or get any vibe really. You do you. I'll do me.
c) Sometimes I'm caught off guard. I get an internal warning, but I don't always know when to trust it.

5. Are you able to pick up on your friend's moods?

a) Yes, it's easy. I can pick up how they're feeling or sense something is just off.
b) I try not to intrude.
c) Sometimes I notice, but I try not to get involved if they don't want to talk about it.

6. When you get a hunch to take action, do you immediately follow through?

a) Absolutely. I regret it when I don't.
b) I go with the flow, choosing not to rock the boat.
c) I sense ideas or suggestions, but don't feel comfortable doing anything about it. I don't want to make a mistake.

7. How do you feel about making decisions?

a) It's a natural part of me. I get a strong sense knowing that I know, so decisions are easy.
b) Are you kidding? So many choices!
c) I can see advantages to both sides and sometimes one seems to stand out.

8. When hearing a story, do you have an automatic sense of the outcome?

a) I'm a walking "spoiler alert." I totally feel it and am correct.
b) I don't like to get involved so I ignore any sense I get.
c) Sometimes I feel "uh-oh" or "yay" but thought it was a coincidence.

9. "Vibes" are weird, wacky, and a product of the 1960s.

a) *No way! Vibes are groovy. Seriously. They're helpful and I connect with mine.*

b) *Vibes are definitely weird and wacky! I totally agree.*

c) *I'm not really sure what "vibes" are.*

10. Do you ever sense that this moment happened before?

a) *All. The. Time.*

b) *No. Deja-vu is just not true.*

c) *I have shades of familiarity with this concept.*

11. Did you ever notice when you hang with certain people, they seem to bring you down or leave you exhausted?

a) *I do. Even reading their text messages will drain me.*

b) *I don't let people impact my moods or energy.*

c) *Interesting. Now that you mention it, yes that does happen.*

12. Have you ever experienced jitteriness, goosebumps, or tightening in your stomach before something happened?

a) *Yes, that's how I know to be alert and pay attention.*

b) *I sense it occasionally but tend to ignore it.*

c) *I have but I just don't know what to do about it.*

13. Have you seen white circles or orbs in your photos?

a) *Yes, and very often they're near me.*

b) *I haven't looked. What's an orb?*

c) *Oooh, I should go check.*

14. Does it ever seem like a flash of light passes in your peripheral vision?

a) *Yes, and it's really distracting!*

b) *Not that I've noticed.*

c) *Maybe?*

15. Have you ever dreamed about someone you loved so very much who has died, and you felt happy or energized when you woke up?

a) Yes, and it was wonderful.

b) No, I don't remember any of my dreams.

c) I thought it was just wishful thinking.

16. Have you ever noticed a random scent like a flower essence, cigarette smoke, or perfume when nothing is around?

a) I do pick that up!

b) No. When I do notice, I see the source of the smell.

c) There are times when I pick up a subtle scent, but I always thought I was just not seeing the source.

17. Do you experience and recognize magical things around you or happening to you?

a) Magic seems to be everywhere around me!

b) There is always a logical reason when things happen.

c) Sometimes I see it for others, not as much or as often for me.

18. Do you frequently sense that someone is watching over you, helping protect you and guide you?

a) I know I have angels protecting me.

b) No, maybe they got lost?

c) There are times I definitely sense them around and then other times when I actually forget about them.

19. I know I have a Sixth Sense. I hear it, trust it and act on it.

a) It's as big a part of me as my breath.

b) That's weird stuff.

c) I do get hunches, I'm just not sure what to do with them.

20. Do you believe in God or in an Infinite Intelligence?

a) Yes.

b) No.

c) Sort of, maybe.

Phew, great job!

Now just to remind you, it's time to tally your scores based on mostly a's, b's and c's.

I can't wait to see what you got!

The Results are IN!

If you answered mostly "**a**" – You're an **Intuitive Savant**!

You intuitively hear messages all of the time. You've got that special connection with the Universe. You're ready to enhance your gifts and confidently take action. Way to go, you manifestor! These 45 days are going to be a fun way to reinforce what you know and kick it up several more notches!

If you answered mostly "**b**" – You're an **Intuitive Ignorer**.

You've got the gift of intuition. You sense your gut feelings, but you prefer to be able to explain it by logic, solid facts and science. But you are still intuitive! You have a quiet inner knowing that has made you a success thus far. Now you are ready to understand and apply your natural gifts and can look forward to getting proven results.

If you answered mostly "**c**" – You're an **Intuitive Hula Hooper**.

You recognize your gifts. You know there's something more going on in the Universe. You're excited to gain more insight, to learn how to hear your intuition and confidently take action. You sense this is the perfect timing to fine-tune your hunches and to remember and utilize the forgotten tools of the universe.

CONGRATULATIONS!

Whatever your score, you already know you have incredible gifts. Now it's time to sharpen your sixth sense and have some real fun! WOOHOO!!!

How to use this book

First, trust yourself.

Second, have fun.

If you already have been exploring your intuition and understand the foundational basics of vibration, grounding and protection, then go ahead and begin the exercises.

And, even if you do already have the core experience, you may want to read through in case there's something new or just for review.

Once you get to the exercises, you can do them sequentially or as your intuition dictates.

The point is practice, practice, practice.

It's like vocal workouts. The more you sing your scales and do your facial warm ups, the stronger your vocal cords. The more you practice listening, trusting and working your intuitive muscle, the stronger your intuitive voice.

Your intuitive muscle is going to love these workouts! And, so are you!

INTUITION ESSENTIALS

Setting your intention

Being clear on your intention alerts the universe and yourself that you are ready and committed to your super powers!

Intention begins with inspiration or divine thought. The universe holds the space for the intention to manifest. Just like an acorn is programmed to become an oak tree.... we are programmed for success.

1. Set your intention. For example: "It is my intention to reinforce, expand and enhance my intuition."

Now, write yours.

2. Create an affirmation from your intention. For example: "I am reinforcing, expanding and enhancing my intuition."

Now, write yours.

3. Visualise success. Close your eyes for 30 seconds, smile and imagine celebrating you are an intuitive super hero.

Remember!
The journey to
manifesting
your dreams
**begins with
intention.**

Before we dive into the daily exercises, I just want to share a few things that can help ensure you are looking after yourself and your energy throughout this process.

First, let's talk about Grounding.

Maybe you already know of this and it will serve as a reminder. Maybe this is a new topic. Either way, I'm here to guide you through it.

What is Grounding?

Grounding is a technique that helps you reconnect with the present moment, especially when things get overwhelming. Think of it like a mental timeout, where you step back, breathe, and center yourself.

You know that feeling when you're kinda all over the place and your mind's racing a mile a minute? Grounding is like hitting the pause button. It's all about bringing yourself back to the present moment, connecting with the here and now.

It's kinda like when you take off those tight shoes after a long day, wiggling your toes and moving your feet, letting all the stress melt away, *that* sensation of truly connecting with the immediate moment. That's what grounding does for your mind. It's like a reset button, helping you to feel more balanced, clear-headed, and ready to tackle whatever comes next. It's like a mental deep breath, getting you centered and focused.

How do we ground ourselves?

I like to begin with a healthy **cleansing breath**, the deep belly kind.

Settle where you are. You may be sitting, standing or reclining. You may be on the floor, in a chair, in a bed, in front of a sink, in the shower, on a beach... wherever you are, allow your body to release tension and relax.

Gently shut your eyes. It's like you're hitting the "mute" button on the world for a teeny bit.

Next, take a deep inhale. Imagine you're smelling the most delicious food or the scent of your favorite flower. Breathe in through your nose slowly for about 4 seconds (or whatever feels right!) letting your belly fully expand...

Hold that breath in for a second or two (or whatever works for you)... No rush, no stress.

Next, exhale like you mean it, letting that breath out slowly through your mouth open, incorporating a sigh. Release this for about 6 seconds.

 Sighing on the exhale helps you hear your release, relaxes your face, jaw, and shoulders.

Dive into this breathing rhythm a few more times, or as many as you need. With each cycle, imagine the day's stress melting away, like butter on warm toast.

And that's it! It's like giving your mind and body a mini-vacation. You can do this anytime, anywhere. A cleansing breath helps you tune in and be present to this immediate moment. It also helps release tension, distractions, concerns and anything occupying your mind keeping you from relaxation. So, the next time the world feels a tad too noisy or chaotic, remember your trusty deep breathing trick. It's like a warm, comforting hug for your soul!

Another, amazing tool you to use is **Centering.**

What is Centering?

Centering is aligning with your inner self and finding that sweet spot of balance and calm within.

All the distracted internal thoughts (laundry list of to-dos, random reminders, wondering if you're going to be bothered or win some mega millions lottery) and external sounds (noticing the neighbor's rooster again, the truck going by, tv in the other room or a text alert) gets zipped up.

Mentally, all that internal and external chatter is zipped up and silenced.

How to Center

Start with a deep, cleansing breath. (You can flip a couple pages back if you want a refresher on this).

While exhaling, deliberately ground yourself, noticing the contact with the Earth.

As your attention connects to the ground, allow any thoughts or distractions to drift away.

At this point, all distractions are eliminated. When you open your eyes, you are present in the here and now.

It's like going into a safe cave. Since your eyes are closed, all of your other senses are heightened. There's a marvelous feeling of peace and tranquility. When you're out of the cave, you feel refreshed and ready.

Finally, I'd like to share another tool I would recommend whenever you are "tuning in." Protection is something you might not be aware of but it's so important to protect your energy.

Protection – What is it?

Protection is an invisible energetic shield. This blocks all unseen harm, ill thoughts, negative emotions and vibrations, and energetic and physical pollution. This barrier keeps your vibration pure.

When to use:

All the time. This is especially when interacting or when being touched by another like a massage therapist or your hairdresser.

Protecting Your Brightness and Lightness

Once you develop clear intuition, you will notice your inner vibration will change and increase in strength. There is something different about you as you begin to listen to and follow your intuition.

> *Once you develop clear intuition, you will notice your inner vibration will change and increase in strength.*

You become lighter and brighter physically, mentally, emotionally, and spiritually. You begin to shine. It's like that natural glow pregnant women get or that delightful feeling people in love radiate. You become a vibrant, beautiful presence.

Unfortunately, in the same way that bright light attracts moths, your bright light will begin to attract everyone and everything. People will naturally be attracted to you and want to be around you because they'll feel fabulous in your presence.

They may not understand the sensation because it can be so subtle, but it'll be evident to their subconscious, and they'll want to be with you. Just by being with you they will notice a boost in their vibration. They'll feel better, lighter and happier. Who doesn't want that, right?

Fortunately, you have the ability to choose the folks you want to share your energy, vibration, and sunshine with. To protect your soul's light, energy and vibration, and let in only the people you want, I recommend that you do a visualisation with a protective bubble which acts like an invisible protective shield. Once completed, this bubble will remain and not interfere with your daily activities.

In this visualisation, you'll be imagining yourself in

a translucent bubble with a screen filter. Anything that would lower your vibration or energy is filtered out, unable to connect with you. Anything made up of love and high vibration will be able to smoothly flow and connect with you.

Read through and then create. You can, also, record the steps into your phone's voice memo and play to keep your eyes shut while doing this.

(You can also access my free recording at **intuitionbreakthroughbundle.com***)*

A super cool thing to note.

The more you do this and become comfortable, the more angels will interact with you. You'll notice angels adding different variants unique to your personality or energy or current situation.

For example, if you're going through a rough patch, you may notice more yellow for courage. If you're about to give a presentation, you may notice angels weaving in music or shades of blue.

Personalized bubbles become a wonderful daily habit. If you're already doing a daily protection visualization then just ask angels to incorporate some of this technique too.

DOING YOUR OWN PROTECTIVE VISUALIZATION

Begin by getting comfortable.

Close your beautiful eyes.

Next, take a cleansing breath (inhaling through your nose for 4
counts and exhaling through an open mouth for the count of 7).

Close your eyes and imagine your angels constructing
a translucent, pink bubble in front of you.

Imagine angels shining light and love into the bubble.

Watch as the bubble expands and shimmers as they fill it
with energy, love, joy, gratitude, wisdom and peace.

When you're ready, imagine yourself stepping into this pink bubble.

Know that you are safe.

Take a cleansing breath, allowing yourself to adjust
and connect with this energetic frequency.

Know that you are able to move completely and at ease.

This bubble is comfortable and unobtrusive.

You can forget about it and go about your daily activities.

Feel yourself relax in your bubble knowing
you are safe and protected.

Gradually allow yourself to come back to your
fully alert self and open your eyes.

Know that the protective barrier will stay
with you throughout your day.

Most intuitive people do this quick protective visualization at the
beginning of each day. This can also be repeated throughout your day
at any time you wish.

Drawing Out Even More Protection

Another fun way to help strengthen and internalize this protection is to draw an image below of yourself in your own bubble.

Use colors and details to make it your own and depict yourself very happy, safe and loved within your very own bubble.

And now you have learnt the three ways you can take care of your energy generally; it is time to take a dive into our journey together.

Are you ready?

I am!

Let's go! I'll be right with you every skip, hop, and jump of the way!

SECTION

02

CONNECTING WITH YOUR INTUITION EVERY DAY!

This section is all about you.

Now you can really put into practice everything we have covered so far, and you can start intentionally connecting with your intuition every day.

There are 45 days of activities that will strengthen your intuition and create the confidence within to trust and take action. Yay!!!!

Most days are achieved in under two minutes. There are some days that you'll be observing your intuition throughout the day. Just do what you can. Relax and enjoy these. It's the most fun you'll have building a muscle!

This book is meant to get dirty. Be written and drawn in. Mark it up. Make it your intuitive interactive sourcebook. Of course, if that feels waaaay too uncomfortable then have a handy nearby designated notebook for tracking your fabulous journey.

You're ready! You can take each day as it comes, or if you feel called to flip through this section of the book to land on a day's activity then go with that too. Look at you already listening and trusting your intuition!

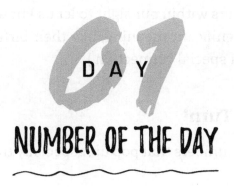

D A Y

NUMBER OF THE DAY

*Day 1 is a fun way to start practicing **listening** to your intuition. Read the description below and then have some fun watching for numbers during your daily activities.*

Numbers!

Sometimes a number seems to be frequently jumping out at you. You may hear people talking about seeing 1111 or 1234 or multiple numbers like 444. You may have, also, noticed this at times, in phone numbers, on a receipt, or wherever, and you chalked it up to coincidence.

But then suddenly, you begin to notice the same number sequence appearing again and again. It pops up on license plates, on your computer, in a random tv scene, in a magazine, and the list goes on. Or every time you look at a clock, you happen to notice the same time over and over. The same numbers stand out.

Guess what??!! *It is a sign.*

You probably already sensed that, didn't you? You're right. And it's a message worth noticing.

Why do I see numbers repeating all around me?

Frequently, angels use numbers to communicate messages, give us encouragement, and to provide a confirmation that they're listening. Sometimes our loved ones who have passed over to the world of spirit put specific numbers within our sight to let us know they are with us. (This often has significant meaning, like their birthday, anniversary or a reference to a special connection.)

Now it's Your Turn!

Today, notice the numbers that pop up, especially those that continue to reappear.

Numbers can be anywhere and everywhere. Set your intention to pick up on specific repetitions or patterns, so you can practice your intuition!

If you feel you've been too busy to notice any numbers or this seems far out of reach, then quietly and sincerely invite angels to show you a sign. You can ask just like you'd ask a friend to help. You can also say the request below.

"Dear angels, please give me signs of encouragement for the topic on my heart. Please help me notice the number or number sequence so that I may interpret your guidance. Thank you so much for your love and assistance."

What number keeps repeating?

Trust your intuition when answering these questions.

What do you feel is the meaning of this number in your life?

What do you feel your angel or the spirit world is trying to convey?

Now that you know there is a significant message being given in numbers let this be a confirmed message of encouragement from your angels!

Angel Number Meanings

On the next few pages, is a list of number meanings that I hand out when teaching my courses and workshops.

This list is of the single digit numbers plus a couple of very common sequences.

When you have a blend of numbers, look at all of the numbers involved when you are interpreting your message. Ask angels for their assistance in clarifying the meaning. You'll sense their response.

Add any additional insight you feel when you see the number or numbers. Listen to your intuition and have fun! Remember, you are communicating with your angels!

Angel Number Meanings

0 – You are directly linked with the Divine. You are connected with the vast Universe. Celebrate your divine connections.

1 – Time for new beginnings! Allow all of your thoughts and energy to nourish you during this precious beginning.

2 – Partnerships! Allow us to assist you in all matters. We are here for you! Ask for our help in balancing all things. This is a great time for your divine path.

3 – Joy! Ascended masters are around you and aiding you. Things are happening! Stay patient, stay happy and allow the right timing to manifest your desires.

4 – Harmony! Angels are here! We've got you covered, baby! Talk to us. Share with us. We want to help and reassure you that you are blessed with all you need to achieve your dreams.

5 – Change! This is a time for healthy choices. Take action for your well-being mentally, physically, spiritually and emotionally. Call on us to help you stay committed to this shift.

6 – Family! Your focus is your family (work, social, home). Be sure to make time for you! Call on us to help you make time for you! Caution! Don't get overwhelmed. Stay focused on your blessings.

7 – Spiritual Awakening! You've got this! Your intuition is open and flowing! Trust it! Invite us to assist in your discernment.

8 – Manifestation! This is time for abundance and prosperity! Have faith. Keep thoughts positive. Lean on us if you need assistance being decisive and keeping your energy up.

9 – Life Purpose! You are doing great! You're on your right soul path. This is a time of exploring your creativity and expression. Keep on keeping on!

10 – God Rocks! Congratulations! You have completed one cycle and it's now time for a new level. Call on us to help balance your power and leadership in this new cycle.

11 – Angel Kisses! We are with you! Sending you love, hugs and kisses. Careful what you think about! You are manifesting at a super speedy rate. You are at the top of your intuitive game!

1111 – Angels are close and listening. Carefully ask for what you want because the angels are poised to take action, and this will manifest quickly.

1212 – You are receiving a vibrational upgrade. This boost will help you work with angels and spirit guides easier. Spiritual work will come easier too!

1234 – Keep putting one foot in front of the other! You are moving onward and upward! Stay on this golden brick path.

444 – Angels are near. You are sensing them, hearing them and working with them. Continue tapping into this connection. You are surrounded with love.

DAY

FLIPPING PAGES TO FIND YOUR ANSWERS

Day 2 is an easy and fast activity that proves your vibration is accurate and that you can tap into your inner wisdom using just about anything – including the nearest book or novel!

Have a question lingering? Need some insight? *Stat?!* Maybe you're sensing an answer but you want some confirmation.

Grab a book. Any book. (I've used everything from the *Bible* to *Big Magic* by Elizabeth Gilbert to the closest spy-thriller.)

While holding your book, sense your question or ask it out loud. *

*Don't worry HOW you're holding your book. The intention for a clear, guiding message is there.

Open the book and let your finger drop to the page.

Read what your finger is pointing to.

Even if you don't have a specific question in mind, do this activity and be open to receiving the answer.

You'll be amazed and surprised at the accurate message.

What Words of Wisdom Did You Discover?

What was your question?

What was the response your finger landed on?

What is your interpretation of this?

How will you act on this?

Now, try it again! And again!

Remember to have an open mind and enjoy the journey! Insights are everywhere.

You've so got this!

DAY 03

POWERING UP YOUR HAND

On Day 3, practice a simple hand position that will immediately boost your intuitive abilities. It's been practiced for centuries in cultures around the world – now it's your turn!

Need a boost to hear your intuitive voice? Easy-peasy. Just power up your hand in this very simple way and feel the burst of good energy!

Touch the tip of your middle finger to the tip of your thumb. Your other fingers are relaxed.

How and Why It Works!

We use our hands to convey messages all the time.

Think about your ability to make a heart with your hands by touching your fingers. Not only is your hand position conveying a message, but you feel it too!

Hand positions that impact our emotional, spiritual and physical body have been around for thousands of years. You can make the most of this ancient knowledge. Let's get started!

This particular hand position boosts your intuitive messages. This hand position is called *Shuni Mudra*. *Mudra* is from the ancient language Sanskrit and means "symbolic and powerful hand gesture." When the two fingers are placed together like this, it encourages patience, discernment, focus, and discipline.

Try this hand position now. Do it a few times and think about it.

What happened when you tried it? Did you feel a tingle or burst of insight or calm? Or something else? Did energy shift around you? Nothing is too small or insignificant, so share every subtle detail.

Now, practice this hand gesture throughout the day whenever you feel your energy dragging or if you need to make a decision or sort through a bunch of things or ideas. It also works well if you're frustrated because it brings you back to the present moment. At the end of the day, think about how it worked and how you felt. What other times might be good to use the *Shuni Mudra*?

D A Y

GIVING YOUR INTUITION A COLOR BOOST!

Day 4 introduces you to using the color blue as a boost to your intuitive senses. Have fun incorporating the color in your daily activities!

There are many words or phrases you can use when you talk about intuitive gifts.

Some people say they get a gut feeling about things or they are accessing their psychic self or their own inner wisdom. Call it a hunch, your Sixth Sense, your third eye – whatever term you use, the color blue naturally resonates with your inner voice.

Today, your task is to give your intuition a boost by incorporating the color blue every way you can.

Here are just a few ideas:

- Wear blue clothing and accessories.

- Use blue ink.

- Eat blueberries.

- Gather photos of your favorite things that are blue and make a collage.

- Get out and take time to enjoy the blue sky.

Feel the difference in your mood and your ability to more clearly sense your intuition when you experiment with more blue in your life!

What ideas or ways did you implement blue throughout your day?

Did certain colors of blue lend more insight than others?

What other ways can you incorporate blue?

Write or draw images of blue things in your life that reflect and reinforce the power of this color and how it is impacting your day.

TAKING STOCK OF YOUR SELF-TALK

Day 5 invites you to think about your self-talk and how it affects you.

Whenever you need to pump yourself up before an interview or a big event, you've probably caught yourself saying to yourself: *"I can do this! I've got this."* Statements like this are great anytime you need strength and encouragement! It's a natural way we boost our confidence.

Remember a time you encouraged yourself. What did you say?

What was the outcome?

Think of other statements you say to yourself on a daily basis. This can be really revealing so be honest. Write them here.

Now go back and circle the positive statements.

How many were not circled?

Think about how many times you slip into negativity about yourself. How can you reword those statements into positive phrases?

"A lot of what we normally say and think is quite negative and doesn't create good experiences for us. We have to retrain our thinking and speaking into positive patterns if we want to change our lives."

– Louise Hay, author, speaker and founder of Hay House, Inc.

Here are some ways to remind yourself to speak kindly and lovingly to yourself:

Affirmation Post-Its: Place sticky notes with positive affirmations or loving messages in areas where you frequently look – on your bathroom mirror, your computer monitor, your refrigerator door, or inside your daily planner. These can say things like "I'm doing great!" or "Remember to speak kindly to myself." (There are additional affirmations for printing at **www.intuitionbreakthroughbundle.com**)

Reminder Alarms: Set alarms or notifications on your phone to go off at specific times during the day. When they sound, take a moment to pause, breathe, and say something loving to yourself.

Wristband or Jewelry: Wear a specific piece of jewelry, like a bracelet or a ring, as your "kindness reminder." Every time you notice it, take it as a cue to say something kind to yourself. You can also use beads or "mindfulness jewelry" that you can touch or fiddle with as a tactile reminder.

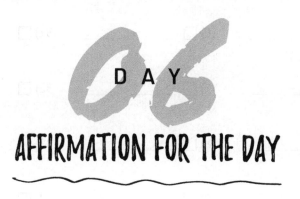

DAY 06

AFFIRMATION FOR THE DAY

Day 6 gives you a powerful affirmation to practice and to remind yourself what you can accomplish when you set your mind to a more positive mindset.

> ## "I am unique, intuitive, and pursue all that is best for me."

Say this affirmation aloud three times every 55 minutes for the whole day.

Set a timer or your phone to alert and remind you.

Check one box each time you say it three times and write a word under the box about how this practice is making you feel.

This will start to train your brain to be positive and supportive about your personal intuitive work.

Try to do it at least 15 times today and see how it feels. That's 45 positive statements just for you!

1) ☐ _____

2) ☐ _____

3) ☐ _____

4) ☐ _____

5) ☐ _____

6) ☐ _____

7) ☐ _____

8) ☐ _____

9) ☐ _____

10) ☐ _____

11) ☐ _____

12) ☐ _____

13) ☐ _____

14) ☐ _____

15) ☐ _____

16) ☐ _____

17) ☐ _____

18) ☐ _____

19) ☐ _____

20) ☐ _____

21) ☐ _____

22) ☐ _____

23) ☐ _____

24) ☐ _____

25) ☐ _____

26) ☐ _____

27) ☐ _____

28) ☐ _____

29) ☐ _____

30) ☐ _____

31) ☐ _____

32) ☐ _____

33) ☐ _____

34) ☐ _____

35) ☐ _____

36) ☐ _____

37) ☐ _____

38) ☐ _____

39) ☐ _____

40) ☐ _____

41) ☐ _____

42) ☐ _____

43) ☐ _____

44) ☐ _____

45) ☐ _____

DAY 07

INTRODUCING MIRROR WORK

Today is all about re-discovering the personal power you gain through offering yourself kindness and self-love on a regular basis.

"I love you."

How is it that those three-little-words seem easier to say to another's face than to your own?

Becoming comfortable in loving ourselves boosts every aspect of our life – including intuition.

Self-respect and self-love help us to celebrate our uniqueness. Confidence seeps into every area of our lives once we start treating ourselves as a cherished best friend.

Intuition is heightened and it becomes quicker, louder and clearer.

Mirror, Mirror

To begin, look in the mirror and smile.

Notice every gorgeous feature.

Now focus on your eyes.

Really look into your beautiful eyes and say, **"I love you. I really do. I love you!"**

Say it with the same level of heartfelt emotion as when you say it to your partner, children, parent, pets, or the love of your life. **"I love you. I really, really love you."**

Let this become a daily routine.

Every time you walk past a mirror, smile and say aloud or mentally: **"I love you."**

If you feel any resistance, just keep trying. It's not always easy to do but it is so transformational. And you **ARE** worth it!

Jot a few notes about the experience below!

How did you feel when you said it for the first time?

As you. Practiced throughout the day, what did you notice? Did it become easier?

Were you naturally drawn to a particular feature of your gorgeous face? Did you notice any new features?

(Even if you spot a wrinkle, blemish or something new that you're not crazy about, acknowledge it. Thank it. Then, visualize your face without that feature. *For example, you spot a new pimple. "Thank you for popping up. I see you and appreciate your message. I will take immediate action loving and accepting myself. Message is received, so you may immediately leave."*

You may be intuitively guided to take an action step of a home remedy, a pimple be gone product, a new face wash or a new food to add to your diet. Your intuition is your go-to bestie for solutions — even face care.

 If you're able, use a dry erase marker and write, "I love you" on your bathroom mirror. This positive message will greet you often, but most importantly, remind you every morning and evening that you are loved.

I Love You

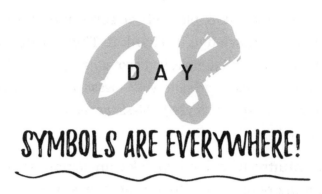

D A Y 08

SYMBOLS ARE EVERYWHERE!

This daily activity encourages you to think about the symbols that are all around you, especially the ones that you tend to see all the time.

Have you seen a butterfly and knew a loved one was near? Have you seen a feather and felt an angel was cheering you on? Do you see a set of numbers and know your wishes are coming true?

Symbols are messages and signs to you. They hold special meaning. Symbols and signs from spirit can be anything, really.

So, think about any kind of letter, shape or number or any sort of animal or natural element. It could be a logo, or any symbol of any kind. You can run into it in your house, at work, outside, on a sign, online — basically anywhere in your field of vision as you go about your daily routines.

Today, draw these images in your own way or write down the words for five to ten objects, symbols or messages that you know invoke a special message to you.

For example, you had a special connection with your Nana who loved ladybugs. Every time you see a ladybug since she's passed, you think of Nana and her encouragement.

Beside each one, record its meaning for you. If you're not sure of the meaning just now, then do your best but don't worry. We're going to develop this skill further as we go along.

Draw here!

1)

2)

3)

4)

5)

Write here!

1)

2)

3)

4)

5)

6)

7)

8)

9)

10)

DAY 09

CREATING YOUR OWN SYMBOL CHART

The activity for Day 9 builds on Day 8 by thinking more about the various general symbols in your life and specifically what they mean to you.

Sometimes we see things and they don't really register as anything significant.

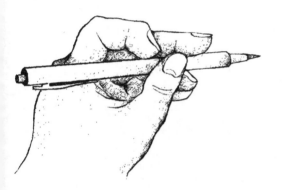

But when you start to identify common objects and the personalized message each one holds for you, you begin creating a series of symbols that your inner voice and angels will be able to use to communicate with you.

Start by asking your intuition to speak up and guide you through this activity.

For each word on the list, draw the image in your own way.

Once you've finished drawing it, write the first thing that comes to mind. Don't overthink it. Just trust your inner wisdom which, as you know, is also called your intuition.

Butterfly

Window

Bird

Dog

Fireworks

Tree

Bike

Book

Door

Ring

Flower

Balloons

Candle

Cat

Hat

Flag

Rainbow

Heart

Add your own personal symbols to your chart and their meanings.

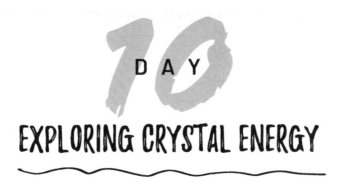

DAY

EXPLORING CRYSTAL ENERGY

Today explores what you know about rocks and crystals and how you can start to use them to enhance your intuitive abilities.

Have you ever spotted a crystal and just loved it? Maybe a diamond caught your attention? A ruby? What about an emerald?

Besides being beautiful and sparkly, crystals have a silent benefit a lot of people don't realize. Crystals have a frequency that vibrates in harmony with many specific topics such as love, wealth, health, and intuition.

Do you have any special rocks or crystals?

What natural elements are you naturally attracted to?

Is it the color or the type?

Have you explored the meaning of crystals before?

Have you felt anything when holding a rock or crystal?

Write about a time when you spotted a rock and slipped it into your pocket, or saw a crystal and it moved you, or had a memorable encounter with a stone.

Do you know what stone it was?

What emotions did you experience with this rock?

Do you still know where it is?

Use colored pencils, markers or crayons and draw your rock below.

DAY 11

USING CRYSTALS TO ELEVATE YOUR INTUITION

Day 11 introduces you to clear quartz which is not only a beautiful crystal but also a powerful tool in the self-development of your intuitive gifts.

Clear quartz is a natural enhancer. It appears in nature as a sparkling translucent type of stone, often with sharp points, resembling an ice crystal. But you may also get it in polished form and many other shapes.

The beauty of clear quartz is that among many wonderful things, it provides clarity to the holder, amplifies energy of other crystals and protects against negativity.

If you have a piece of this, bring it out or purchase one soon so you can begin using it daily. While holding the piece of clear quartz in your hand, set your intention to gain more clarity.

Use this statement, or one like it, to state your intention out loud.

> ## "I am filled with clarity, perfect light, and radiate beautiful love."

What experience did you have with clear quartz when you used it to
set your intention?

Make note of any ideas, feelings, or impressions you got while starting
to work with this crystal.

Slip this crystal into your pocket or keep near you as much as possible
to keep the connection growing!

(Go deeper with your intuitive crystal connection in your bonus at
www.intuitionbreakthroughbundle.com)

D A Y

RECLAIMING AND RETAINING CONTROL

Today's activity reminds you that you have full control over anything you sense is going to happen to you or someone else.

Just because you got a hunch that something bad was going to happen (and it did!) know that *you* didn't *cause* it to happen. Whether you said it aloud before the event or kept it to yourself, you didn't cause that accident or the break-up or whatever it was. Nothing negative occurred because you felt it. And you are not going to bring upon any specific events just by tapping into your intuitive gifts on a regular basis. Phew!!

Can you think of a time when you had a hunch that something was going to occur before it actually did?

How did that experience play out?

Do you feel this experience has since limited or blocked your intuitive gifts?

Are you willing to move past this?

Do you know what steps you can take if you get a negative or worrisome sense? (Don't worry if you don't yet — read on!)

How to protect yourself – and maintain control

If you get a hunch that something bad or harmful might be about to happen:

1) Remember everyone has free will, including yourself. So, you can share your insight that might be a warning, and yet the other person may still go through with it. That is their free will and their choice. But this also gives you the choice to take another direction, using your own free will, if you wish to avoid something unpleasant or harmful that you see in your own path. You are in control.

2) You can place a mental hedge of protection around the other person or yourself through visualization.

3) You can send angels to protect them or call on angels to protect yourself. It's as easy as saying, *"Dear Angels, please protect _____."*

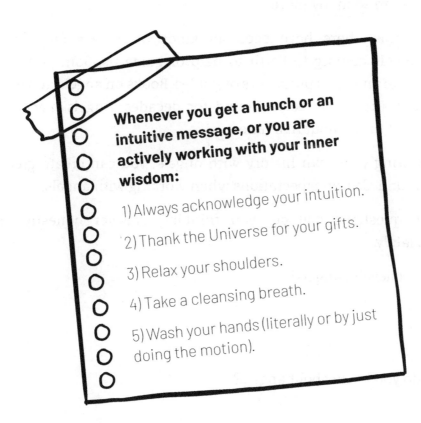

Whenever you get a hunch or an intuitive message, or you are actively working with your inner wisdom:

1) Always acknowledge your intuition.

2) Thank the Universe for your gifts.

3) Relax your shoulders.

4) Take a cleansing breath.

5) Wash your hands (literally or by just doing the motion).

DAY 13

MAKING ANGEL CONNECTIONS

Today's activity invites you to think about angels, how angels have been part of your daily life and how you can strengthen this connection.

Do you remember seeing in picture books or cartoons the image of a person with a sweet angel on one shoulder and a little devil on the other? That is just one way we might see angels depicted in our lives, but there are so many more.

For example, there have been all kinds of movies and shows about angels coming to Earth to help or guide us. Some religions incorporate angels as protectors or guides. Books on angels and angel communication have been around for decades. Angels have been recognized throughout ALL time.

By exploring your own history with angels, you can create greater comfort and clearer expectations when working with angels.

Today's questions will get you thinking. Answer honestly and immediately.

Do you believe in angels?

What do you know about angels?

When were you first introduced to angels?

What were the circumstances?

Have you ever felt angels near? What did you experience?

Have you ever seen sparkling lights or orbs? Or have you noticed any in photos of yourself or photos you took?

Starting to Work with Angels

Ask yourself, are you open to working with angels? If it's a "no" or "not yet," then ask yourself to reveal the cause of your hesitation so you can address and move on. Remember, angels won't barge in or interfere… They need to be asked. If you're ready to work with angelic assistance, begin by inviting them!

Say something like:

"Guardian angels and archangels, it is my sincere desire to work with you. Please help me open and to recognize and trust your presence. Please help me hear your messages for my highest good, and I will follow your guidance. Thank you for helping me bring this to pass."

Now write out your own invitation, in your own words or using the paragraph just suggested:

Notice the handwriting that you just did because even the act of writing can create sensations. Was your handwriting different? Maybe easier to read or just looked different? Maybe you felt a cool or warm breeze? Maybe you suddenly noticed a unique or familiar scent? Maybe an image from years gone by popped into your thoughts? Those subtle observations are signs from your angels.

Write anything you noticed here.

Now add any images, colors, thoughts, words, names and insights you experienced about this or that come to you during the rest of the day.

Partnering with angels in your daily life is like having celestial co-pilots on your life's journey. Not only do they offer an accurate guidance for your soul, ensuring you don't miss spiritual signs, symbols and messages, but they also supercharge your intuition, making everyday decisions feel like a breeze. So, the next time you're at a crossroads, remember: teaming up with angels might just give you the divine nudge you need!"

"*I am convinced these heavenly beings exist and that they provide unseen aid on our behalf.*"

– Reverend Billy Graham, author of *Angels and Angels: God's Secret Agents*

DAY 14

CREATING YOUR OWN COLOR SYMBOLS

Today helps you quickly work out the inner meaning of various colors in your world so you can use them as signs or symbols from your spirit and angel guides.

Best way for today: No overthinking! First reaction and gut feelings only.

Are you ready for the quick-fire round? It's so easy. Next to each color, write down the first thing you think of when you read, hear or say that color. *Go!*

Black ....

Red ....

Yellow ....

Orange ....

Green ....

Pink ....

Blue ....

Purple ....

White ....

HOORAY!!!! You just created color symbols you can watch for and work with every day! When you ask angels for clarification, ask for a color confirmation.

Notice what color suddenly appears.

Your intuition will supply the interpretation.

(For example, let's say pink reminds you of a girl, precious and sweet. Then, you asked angels if you should explore this job opportunity. Suddenly a person wearing a pink backpack passes you, you'd intuitively feel it's a yes. It's a sweet opportunity. Girls are precious and this opportunity will be too!)

Work with this throughout your day. Notice any colors that pop up in your mind's eye, draw your attention or seem to be frequently reappearing. Were you able to receive their messages?

BONUS! *Use colored pencils, markers or crayons to color the corresponding color next to each word.*

For example:

   Purple

DAY 15

FEELING ENERGY IN YOUR HANDS

This is a quick and fun hands-on activity in which you can feel fields of energy and notice how it shifts and changes.

We clap. We wave. We hold hands.

The palms of our hands have energy which is easy to feel.

Start by rubbing your palms together for about 10 to 15 seconds and then move your hands apart three or four inches as if cradling a round invisible ball that is very delicate.

Feel the energy as it pings across from palm to palm, up your fingers and back to the palms of your hands. Hold your hands steady and concentrate until you really feel it. (You may feel the sensation of swirling energy, tingles, cold or warm air or warmth in your hands)

Once you've established the flow of energy, begin to play with the ball by moving your hands as if you really had a ball in your hands. Imagine it growing in size as by moving your hands apart. Compress your ball by moving your hands closer together. Move your hands around while playing with the energy of your ball.

Next, hold your energy ball in a comfortable size and speak your verbal desires directly to the ball. You can include desires such as love, insight, clarity, joy, gratitude, health, and angel connections. Notice how your energy ball increases in size as it absorbs each word spoken into it.

When you feel your ball is perfectly filled and you're ready to manifest, bring your hands and the imaginary ball toward your heart and allow the ball to release into your chest.

Now notice your immediate physical shift as the energy from your ball becomes one with your heart.

What shifts did you notice?

Write down here the things that you chose to put into your ball.

In what other ways are you aware of invisible energy fields in your life?

Continue to think about the things that you desired and that you put in your ball in order to manifest them. Watch for signs during the day and week that indicate those desires are becoming real for you.

DAY

EATING THE BEST TO BOOST YOUR CLARITY

Today you'll be thinking about what you eat each day and practice using your intuition to help you make the best food choices for you and your body. WOOHOO!!!

Food is something we all need but in today's world, making the right food choices can be confusing and overwhelming. There is so much information and *misinformation* out there.

Your intuition is an excellent guide to help you make the best and healthiest choices. You just have to learn to work with it and trust what it tells you.

Today is your chance to become more aware of the relationship between what you eat and drink and how those things make you feel.

Foods that Give You a Mixed-up Sluggish Feeling

Check in with yourself at a point today when your intuition or gut feeling just doesn't seem right. It might be fuzzy, you might be really uncertain about a decision, or you might have a spinning feeling or be in a sluggish state.

In the midst of this unsettled feeling, think about what you might have been eating or drinking right before this muddle-up occurred.

For example, was it a heavy meal? Was it too much caffeine? Did you just try some new food or spice you were not used to? Did you stop for fast-food and scarf it down in the car? Or maybe you didn't eat enough, and you found yourself feeling faint and fuzzy?

Time to play food detective! Make a few notes below about how food affects you today. Also add any foods you know don't agree with you.

How did your food choices affect your mood?

Is there a pattern to these foods?

Are they linked to your emotions or spiritual balance?

Have you noticed certain foods impacting you only when you don't meditate or get off your spiritual practice?

Are you able to easily eat whatever you want when you feel joyous and grateful?

Let your sleuthing reveal your soul and body talk!

Foods that Get You Clear and In the Zone

Now think about the times when you are completely in the flow of life, all cylinders working well, when your intuition is on high alert!

What kinds of foods were you consuming just before this awesome feeling? What gave you the good vibe buzz that makes you an Intuitive Rock Star? Maybe fresh food choices, might be lots of water, might be your own brand of comfort food — whatever it is, make a note of the things that keep you on your toes, alert, happy, in the zone, and trusting your intuition.

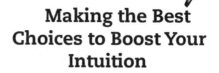

Making the Best Choices to Boost Your Intuition

Organic and fresh are good choices for intuition clarity.

Raw pineapple and blueberries are more than just a sexy, yummy treat. You'll find they give you a zing, too! Try adding almonds for a boost. Leafy, green veggies really sweeten your intuitive vibe, too.

If you happen to be having a super psychic kind of day then adding some organic oats or eggs to your diet helps. A smoothie with a bit of protein for the shift too. My go-to after a reading event? Dark chocolate.

Use what you've learned today about yourself and your relationship between food and mood to make your own go-to top food choices, then keep them handy when you need them. Add to this list and see if you spot any patterns appearing.

My Top 5 Foods and Drinks for Clarity

1) ....

2) ....

3) ....

4) ....

5) ....

DAY 17

ENERGETICALLY CLEANSE YOUR FOOD

Today is about food too, but this time think about the energy that is in and around the food you consume. Learn how to clear excess energy so you don't get a negative whammy that you didn't see coming.

It's not just the food that you eat that impacts your energy levels, it's all of the vibrational energy that those food items picked up along the way.

The lesson today is to *cleanse* your food before munching. And this concept is about more than rinsing and cleaning your veggies and fruit under water, although that is a good idea!

What I'm talking about is the food and liquid you consume —meat, plant protein, dairy, snacks, restaurant food, vegetables, water, soda, and wine you drink. Everything you consume has an energetic vibration that it picked up in its journey to your plate, your fork or your glass.

Was your barista this morning in a foul mood? It could have rubbed off into your coffee or tea.

Were the snacks you just ate mass produced in a huge factory? Those simple treats might have picked up any of thousands of vibrations from the people and machines where they were made. Did the banana you just peeled come from half-way around the world? YIKES! Just imagine the handling and influences it came under on its long trek to your hand. In each case, the food is carrying more than just nutrition!

Fortunately, there are ways to keep that excess energy or negative energy from impacting you in a negative way. Here are some clearing techniques you can practice today to see which ones work best for you! Once you find what you like, that really gives you a clean and clear feeling with your food choices, then use that with your food all the time.

Three Quick Ways to Clear Your Food and Drink

1) Say a blessing over your food. Even a simple statement said aloud or to yourself can clear any unwanted energy from what you are about to consume. So, you can say, *"Bless this food and those who prepared it, allow it to be used only for our highest and greatest good."* Or *"Bless this."*

2) Clear foods with your hands by placing your hands, palms down, over the top of your food, with the intent to remove any and all unwanted and unneeded energetic vibration from it. You can imagine gold rays shining down upon your food and cleansing away any negativity.

3) Use the *Seven Circles* technique. This one can be done above the table or below the table discreetly, if you just want to be private about your clearing efforts.

Use your hand to draw seven circles rotating clockwise over your plate of food or below the food plate under the table and while you do this, visualize any negativity gathering and being pulled off the food. Imagine it all gathering into your fingers, and toss that excess energy to the floor, discarding it.

Try these things each time you consume food or drink today and make some notes as to how it felt and how you felt afterwards. Think about how you can make this an everyday habit.

I ate/drank this: | I applied this technique: | I felt this:

I ate/drank this: | I applied this technique: | I felt this:

I ate/drank this: | I applied this technique: | I felt this:

I ate/drank this: | I applied this technique: | I felt this:

I ate/drank this: | I applied this technique: | I felt this:

Did you notice yourself intuitively choosing one technique repeatedly? Which was it?

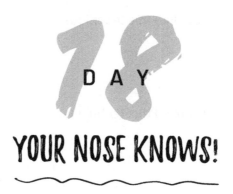

DAY 18

YOUR NOSE KNOWS!

Today is when you learn about how your sense of smell works to enhance your intuitive abilities.

Have you ever noticed a smell and there's nothing and no one around? Could be a sweet smell or something strong and awful, could be anything.

Maybe it's the smell of coffee but there isn't anyone brewing or sipping anywhere near you. Or you might suddenly smell your father's cigarette smoke and yet no one near you is smoking. Or out of the blue, you get a whiff of your grandmother's perfume that you haven't smelled since she passed.

Maybe you just walked by some flowers and that scent was like her perfume and it was to remind you of her love for you! Perhaps you were rushing to your car and got a whiff of some smelly trash from nowhere in particular, and you realized, "Oh snap! Forgot to put out the garbage."

Your senses all convey messages and feelings to you, but most times, we are not even aware of it. Some might seem obvious, but others are very subtle. Today, it's time to get your 50 million olfactory receptors super active by noticing scents all around you.

Just pretend you're like a beagle sniffing out your world. Beagles are the superstars at this because they have 45 times more receptors in their noses than we do! Woof! Woof!

Learn to Notice What Your Nose Knows

Step One:

Before you set out, state out loud your intention clearly with this kind of an affirmation:

"I notice and appreciate every scent that drifts my way. I clearly understand the message in each scent."

Step Two:

Then sniff out everything you encounter, seen and not seen! Make note of what you discovered and how it made you feel. Think about what the meaning could be to you and why it appeared when it did. Try to notice at least four different scents today and make some notes below.

I smelled _____ when I was _____

and I felt this _____.

I smelled _____ when I was _____

and I felt this _____.

I smelled _____ when I was _____

and I felt this _____.

I smelled _____ when I was _____

and I felt this _____.

I smelled _____ when I was _____

and I felt this _____.

Step Three:

As you ponder each scent, think about whether the message was a cautionary scent or a reminder of something or someone important.

Did it fill you with peaceful feelings or dread? Why do you think it came to you just then? What action do you think this scent was suggesting to you?

Add to your notes above.

DAY 19

HUGGING A TREE

Time to go outside to find a great place to get grounded and feel the immense power of Mother Earth.

Trees are grounding, helpful and beautiful. They help reduce stress and anxiety even by just looking at a photo of them. Being outside near trees boosts our immune system and creates a sense of belonging, joy and an overall *life is good* vibe.

Research has proven the benefits and in 1982, Japan launched a national program of Tree Bathing. This consists of no screen time, just green time. Walking through the forest and enjoying the company of trees.

You don't have to go to Japan to enjoy the physical, mental, and spiritual benefits. Today's exercise connects you with this gentle and extremely powerful healing in your own local space.

1) Head outside and proceed to the closest tree.

2) Run up and hug it! (You don't have to actually run. Maybe saunter? Sashay? Skip? Moonwalk? Mosey?)

3) Wrap your arms around its base and feel the strength flowing through it.

4) Notice the bark, the leaves, the branches.

5) Feel the power and the love.

6) Thank the tree for sharing its beauty and calming presence.

Now draw the tree you just met with.

What type of tree did you choose?

What did you feel and experience?

How did this feel physically?

What did you hear? Leaves rustling, birds singing, etc.

What did you intuitively sense?

DAY

MAKING YOUR OWN SACRED SPACE

It's an inside day today on Day 20 and this is an invitation for you to create a special and sacred place in your home that honors you and your inner growth. The space you create can be anything you want it to be!

This is your chance to build a nice space for yourself that is dedicated to you and things you like, things that uplift your spirit and remind you of your inner divinity.

We are all children of the Universe or God or Divine Creation, whatever you want to call it. The space you create is not about a given religion or set of beliefs but rather it's just a safe and serene place where you can breathe, feel at peace and be spiritually connected.

Don't worry, there are no right or wrong things here, it's whatever you like. It doesn't have to be a whole room that you dedicate to this purpose — it could just be a corner, a little nook, a shelf, a windowsill, or a small table. Use what you have.

Your sacred space is a prepared area that you designate specifically for grounding, creating, and connecting with Divine Intelligence.

This will be where you can go to feel safe, loved, and inspired. Ideally it should be a space that is personal and private.

This spot is energetically charged by your intention and the items you choose to keep there. The space doesn't have to be huge and it doesn't have to make sense to anyone but you. This is your space.

How to Prepare your Sacred Space:

1) Select a spot you can dedicate to this purpose.

2) Wash the area with vinegar and water or your favourite cleanser.

3) Once dry, place a silk scarf or special cloth on it that you like. (Refer to your color meanings from Day 14 if you're wanting to add specific energy). If you intuitively feel like skipping this step, then skip it!

4) Consider items you'd like to include, such as trinkets or crystals, that have meaning to you.

5) Use items you may have collected from your travels or kept from childhood like photos, charms, buttons, or favorite stuffed animals.

6) Add your items to your space.

7) Add candles if you're able or perhaps incense.

8) Consider adding scents. Essential oils such as frankincense and myrrh have high vibration and boost intuition.

Where will you create your sacred space?

Sketch out your ideas and items here that you would like for your sacred space. Be open to the intuitive insight you receive while doing this! Your instincts will know or suddenly recall an item that will be a perfect addition!

Place a photo here!

How to Use Your Sacred Space:

The way you interact with your space is completely up to you. You may just want to use it as a visual reminder to stop and be present as you go about your daily activities. You might kneel beside it or meditate in front of it.

Whenever you might need to have a heart-felt conversation with your inner self, you can do this in your sacred space. If you have an important decision you need to make, your space is the ideal place to consider it. Or you might just use your space as a quiet time location where you can curl up with a good book while enjoying the peace and serenity.

Whatever you create, trust your inner guidance, *your* intuition. Place what and where you want. This is your intimate creation. No one else's. You can change, adjust or move it any time you want. Your sacred space is YOUR sacred space.

*(Discover more ideas at **www.intuitionbreakthroughbundle.com**)*

D A Y 21

CANDLE GAZING

Today you'll amplify your clairvoyance (intuitively clear seeing) through a simple tranquil activity that anyone can do. All you need is a candle, a way to light it, a timer or alarm to set, and some quiet time.

This is a great exercise for boosting your clairvoyance and focus during meditation.

Clairvoyance is the ability to perceive things around you or events in the future that are beyond normal sensory contact.

Through the practice of watching the flame, you develop a laser-keen focus and it helps turn up your intuitive volume.

Here are the steps:

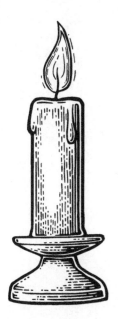

1) Light a candle.

2) Sit comfortably about 10-18 inches away.

3) Set your timer for 2 - 5 minutes.

4) Gaze at the flame.

5) Focus on the teeny tiny blue part of the flame. Watch it dance, fluid in motion.

6) Imagine an invisible string reaching out from the flame connecting with the center of your forehead.

7) Keep the connection as you enjoy the dance of the flame.

Your forehead may feel tickly or itchy. You may feel mesmerized. You may feel bored. Try to stick with it.

If the time is just too long, try to set the time first for 30 seconds and then increase it the next time to one minute. Once you are used to that, you can then add minutes to the next time.

After your timer notifies you that your time for the meditation is up, write your experience here.

Think about what you felt, what messages you received, or how your clarity or confidence improved or felt different than usual.

Save your candle for another activity later!

DAY 22

EXPLORING YOUR SENSE OF TASTE

It's your chance to tickle your taste buds and develop a greater awareness of clairgustance (extra sensory perception of taste). What could those tastes be telling you?

Today it's your chance to notice the flavor of everything you eat, drink or observe. You may be thinking, "I get the eat and drink, but *observe?*"

Yes!

Whenever you walk into an office, you may notice the aroma of coffee and your mouth salivates. You may see a banana and your mouth senses "mushy-like baby food," and then a memory pops up! For me, bananas are a happy connection because my mind always thinks of my dog, Honey. She's totally my girl and totally loves bananas. Some of my cutest memories of her are from us sharing bananas.

There are symbols and messages hidden in your memories and taste buds.

For example, a certain taste might give you the sense that a loved one is around you in spirit and you feel comforted.

Or maybe your taste buds might be telling you that something is slightly "off" with a food item and the message combines with your intuition as a warning not to eat it.

In another case, you might experience a bitter taste and it's not about the food itself but rather about something bitter you are holding on to that you need to forgive.

Figuring Out What the Flavors Mean

Today, write down the flavors you experience, what you feel and any notes you can add about memories or associations you have about this particular taste sensation.

Taste	Feeling	Memories or Meaning

DAY 23

HEAR THE MEANING BEHIND THE SOUNDS

Another super-sensory day. Today you'll work with your clairaudience (extra sensory perception of sound). You'll be heightening your awareness of the sounds around you. Instead of tuning out background sounds, begin to pay attention and think about what insights those sounds have for you.

There are so many layers of sound around you all day but most of them are tuned out. Think about all the background noise such as music, nature, traffic, and the electronic hum of all our devices. In conversations, you may sense emotions and messages you don't actually hear but the nuance is there. At work, you might hear background sounds as a constant drone rather than distinct sounds.

What if for this one day you would say, "I'm going to observe all the sounds I hear." Set your intention to hear more than you would normally hear and get messages you might have been missing.

State your intention affirmation for the day:

"I notice and appreciate every sound that comes my way. I clearly understand the message in each sound."

Then each time you perceive a new sound, write everything down about it, including what you were feeling at the time you heard the sound and what you feel that this sound is telling you.

Sound Heard	Feeling	Memories or Meaning

Listening for Personal Meaning

Here are a few examples of how sound can communicate and deliver an intuitive message as shared by some of my students.

- "While walking through the lobby, I heard the elevator-music version of the Star Wars theme. I felt like Obi-Wan was saying the force is strong with me. Go me and my intuition!"

- "I just heard a swoosh of steamed milk from the barista. But, it made me think of this special coffeehouse where I've made so many great memories. I feel like I just got a sign that everything is going to work out."

- "This morning, I heard blue jays squawking loudly like they were calling each other. I felt excited. Feeding the birds with my grandpa is a cherished memory. I totally feel like my grandpa was squawking along with those birds, cheering me on and telling me it is time for me and my dreams to fly!"

- "While walking down the street, I passed a place my ex and I used to always hang out. I was considering calling my ex. Phone in hand, suddenly, I heard a car alarm going off. Okay! That warning was loud and clear!"

- "I wasn't eavesdropping, however, the two people on the elevator were having a conversation. The teenager exclaimed, 'Oh my stars!' I asked her, 'What did you just say?!' It's the same expression my grandma always used. She repeated and I had heard correctly! Grandma was like my mom. I had been missing her. It really felt like she sent a hug from heaven."

- "That song in the elevator caught my attention! The words were so encouraging. I know it felt like a special encouragement just for me."

Snippets of speech, sounds of nature, lyrics, tv show conversations can all be used to deliver a message and/or confirm your intuition. Trust your ears!

JAMMING TO YOUR OWN DANCE PARTY

It's a day to get moving! Celebrate your body by letting loose to your favorite tune and observe how it can completely change your mood.

Time to crank up your tunes and move it! Twist, hip-hop, grapevine, two-step, sidestep, any step. Do whatever movements feel good or just sway side-to-side. Blast your music or hum your own tune to yourself. The important action of today is to dance. What could be simpler?

Before you get going, just do a 10-second check in on your general mood. Are you bored, tired, distracted, hungry or something else? Make a quick mental note.

Then set your timer for three to five minutes, turn on some tunes and get moving.

What songs were you jamming to?

Why did you pick these?

How do you feel?

Dance Party Pick-You-Up

Take a few moments to rate your alertness before you got your groove on compared to afterward. How did you feel while moving? Did any muscles stand out? Did any memory ping for you?

Record some notes here about your experience and know that you can use this simple technique to shift your mood or get you started any time your energy seems to be low.

Extra Credit!

Throughout the day, keep your fluid motion going. Sway while standing in line. Tap your fingers. Strike a dance pose just because you can! Keep a melody playing all the time and keep that movement going. It's a beautiful thing!

DAY 25

I SPY WITH MY LITTLE EYES... EVERYTHING!

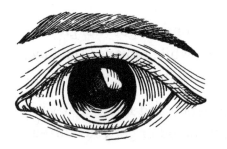

With your eyes wide open and all senses tingling, it's time to notice things at a deeper level and see what has been hiding in plain sight.

It's all about observation today and using all your senses to pick up on what is going on around you. Set the intention to pick up on even the slightest things that you see, hear, smell, taste, touch, or sense. You'll be employing all of your extra sensory perceptions! Intuition bonanza!

As you go about this day, pick one of your usual settings and tune in, noticing all that you can.

Try to stay quiet so all your senses can be tuned in. If you're able, don't engage in conversation. Turn your electronics off. Blend in and listen. Crank up your intuitive antenna.

Stay observing as long as you can. If you can only do five minutes, that's okay! Able to go fifteen minutes? Woohoo! Thirty? Super stellar and super hero status!

Journal all the things you noticed, especially the surprising ones.

Think about what you learned about yourself, your life and your surroundings from doing this.

What did you experience overall? Was there one prominent theme or message that seemed to stand out?

Fun Ways to Amp It Up!

Close your eyes or cover them with a blindfold. Listen deeper. Home in on one sound or sensation. How is your body responding? What are you feeling? Sensing?

Now try it with headphones or anything that blocks sound. What do you notice? See? Feel? How are things altered? Or is it the same?

DAY 26

FINDING WISDOM THROUGH AUTOMATIC WRITING

Connect with your own inner wisdom through good old handwriting. Through the power of the pen, you can tap into guidance and answers you desire.

This simple technique has so many wonderful benefits! This opens the door to your soul's communication and it's a great way to connect with spirit guides!

To get started, make sure you're relaxed and feeling grounded. You can do this right before you fall asleep, when you first wake up, or at any quiet moment within your day.

Imagine protective, loving white light encircling you. Say a simple prayer of protection and gratitude in advance, such as:

> *"I am surrounded by the Universal light of love and protection. Let nothing enter or be received except that which is of pure light and love. Let all messages be easy to understand and for the good of all. Thank you."*

Let your mind relax, let your eyes droop or completely close. Take a cleansing breath.

Ask your angels or your inner wisdom to share a message with you and start writing.

You may see a symbol. Draw it.

You may hear a message. Write it.

You may feel sensations or emotions. Record what you feel.

You may notice smells. Write them.

Write down everything you sense in whatever way it comes.

Don't take time to edit your work or try to be perfect about it. No critiquing or judgements here, just write or sketch what you sense. Be confident that you are establishing a connection and communication style and allow it to flow. No worries if you write off the page, misspell anything or feel silly. This is fun and truly the beginning of a loving relationship.

When you feel your messages are all recorded, say thank you and set the pages aside for a bit of time as you return to your usual state of mind.

Ways to Wrap up and Get More

Take a break after your writing exercise and go back to your pages after a bit of time when you can look at it fresh. Again, no judgements or worries, just look at the words or sketches and see what insights or specific actions were recommended.

Then ask yourself how and when you will follow up on this inner wisdom and take action. What steps could you take today to get started? Make a few notes here to keep yourself on track.

I'd like an Automatic Answer, Please!

Try this same exercise when you need specific advice. Just before you begin the automatic writing part, state a specific question you wish to have answered or a specific situation that you would like clarity about. Write it down at the top of the page and have confidence that the answer is within you and around you.

So you could ask something like:

"Should I continue to date the man (or woman) I met last month?"

"Is it time to find a new job and if so, where do I start?"

"Why can't I seem to get started on my book — what's holding me back? I'm on a deadline."

"Why is there such a deep divide between me and my brother-in-law and what can I do about it?"

Take a deep breath and allow your thoughts to flow onto the paper. Review it afterward to gain the insight, direction or clarity you requested. Say thank you, and show your gratitude by acting upon it.

DAY 27

MAKING MORE OF YOUR MINDLESS CHORES

Get more out of your day. While doing general chores, put your extra mind power to work sorting out something important that has been bothering you.

We all have mundane chores: washing dishes, doing laundry, buying groceries, driving to work, and all those little things.

When doing these mindless chores and daily activities, have you noticed you sometimes get the *best ideas*? Doesn't it seem like shower time is a magnificent idea time?

This is because your mind has far more capability than you need at any given time. You can clean or cook and still have lots of capacity in your mind for other things. So why not allow your mind to do its best work while you sort out the laundry or wash the windows? It's a great way to let your natural *overthinking* work for you!

Set your intention to gain knowledge and clarity on a general matter or specific question and then let your thoughts wander while you go about your automatic activities like cleaning or sorting.

If possible, record your voice on your phone or mini-recorder if you're unable to write at that moment. Allow the endless audible stream of automatic thinking to continue. Let your ideas, suggestions, and inspiration flow!

Listen to the messages from your recording at a later time and thank your angels and your inner wisdom for the insights.

By receiving and responding, you can set up the expectation that every time you do that task you will gain further insight and guidance.

And don't forget to say thank you, because each time you express your gratitude and respect for your inner wisdom, it opens your intuitive reception channels even wider.

Make some notes here about your experiences once you've tried this technique and the goodness that came from tapping into your excess mind power.

Did you notice an increase in guidance while doing certain activities?

Look for your intuitive preference. *For example, you may find washing dishes and shower time to be stronger intuitive downloads compared to walking your dog or running on a treadmill. Try this for several days and discover your intuitive flow sweet spot!*

DAY 28

YOUR GUT-BASED GUIDANCE SYSTEM

Get ready for some lessons on how to listen to your gut and give it credit for its magnificent guidance system. The more you use your gut to guide you, the smoother your life will flow.

Our activity for today is literally *a feeling in your gut*. It's like a tightening, slight discomfort, a sinking feeling, or even a rumbling. It isn't because you're hungry or you're constipated. It's literally your intuition giving you a physical sign that something is *not* good. You may feel butterflies or a light feeling for a physical sign that something is great!

Do you remember a time you experienced this? Have you listened and followed this before? Or maybe you ignored the gut-feeling warning and learned the hard way.

Having this built-in guidance system is a golden opportunity to make the best decisions for yourself and your life. Humans on earth used gut feelings to save themselves from harm for thousands of years, so why not tap into it yourself?

Gauging Your Gut Reaction

Here's a good way to start gaging your gut reactions to things. Quiz yourself as you proceed through your day by playing this simple "yes/no" game.

When you hear a specific statement, argument or theory, ask yourself a "yes/no" question and feel the reaction of your stomach.

The question could be: "Is this true?" or "Is this a good idea?"

Recognize your stomach's response when unhealthy choices or negative impacts are being spoken about, suggested or implied throughout your day. You may feel a tightening, a queasy feeling or complete nausea. This would also be receiving a "no."

Alternatively, feel how your stomach is more at ease when good choices or positive impacts are being spoken about, suggested or implied. You may feel bubbles of excitement. This would also be your intuition providing a "yes."

Here are some questions to read aloud to get your gut muscles flexing.

1) I am a girl.
2) I live in Alaska.
3) I have blue eyes.
4) I own the best dog.
5) I am a cat person.
6) My friends love it when I sing.
7) I make the best chocolate chip cookies.
8) I love my job.
9) I play a musical instrument.
10) I love the color blue.

While going through your answers, you may have noticed a 'maybe." Those happen! It's life. Notice how your gut responded to the maybes. Jot that reaction here.

So, you've had a great day or maybe just morning. You've been noticing. Write down some of your experiences with listening to your gut feelings or ignoring them.

"I rely far more on gut instinct than researching huge amounts of statistics."

– Sir Richard Branson, business magnate and entrepreneur.

DAY 29

EXPRESSING YOURSELF

Express yourself and gain further confidence in the fact that you do know a lot of things, seen and unseen. You're already naturally intuitive, so why not express that to the world?

There is so much that you're aware of each day and you already talk about those things in your conversations. Today is your chance to notice your various interactions and how you're expressing yourself.

So, you may just naturally say things like:

- *I feel...*

- *My sense is that ...*

- *That just doesn't feel right.*

- *I can't explain it, but ...*

- *My hunch is ...*

- *My gut says ...*

- *I don't think that person is telling the truth.*

- *Something doesn't sound right.*

- *Still seems foggy. I think I need to wait before making a decision.*

Notice that we often use the word "feel" rather than "know" when we express our intuition.

"Knowing" is a word that comes from your head and is more logical, whereas "feeling" comes from your heart or your gut, and it is like a deep sense of something that might not have logical or scientific support.

However, once you are tuned into your intuition, expressing it and working with it daily, you will have a calm and strong sense of "knowing" things that defy logical explanation.

How Do You Express Yourself?

Today, start to take a closer notice of the phrases you use and also those around you. Which phrase did you state the most?

Think about what happened after that thought or later in the day. Did you notice that you were correct?

Who around you also seemed to express their intuition freely today? Sometimes this might surprise you. Think about it. These people may be kindred souls, helping you watch out for things — even though you might usually think of them as just a co-worker, neighbor, or a service provider whom you only know casually.

Extra Credit:

Did you experience any physical sensations as if confirming an insight that you just said out loud or that you just heard? Did you feel goose bumps ripple up your arms? A tickling of your scalp? Tightness in your stomach? Make a note to watch for these sensations all the time and allow them to guide you.

DAY 30

ENERGIZING GROUNDING

Take time to run through the steps to this simple grounding exercise that you can do anytime you feel light-headed, unfocussed or overwhelmed.

Sometimes you pick up energy that isn't yours.

This grounding technique will calm, energize your soul, and reset any "off" energy.

It's only natural that you are going to run into daily frustrations or a sense of overwhelm sometimes, and it's just as natural to ground yourself and put yourself back in control of your emotions and your life.

This *Standing and Grounding Technique* is a simple and quick way to return to equilibrium when things are piling up and feeling derailed. It boosts your energy, smooths out your emotions, and grounds your vibration.

Standing and Grounding Technique

Stand and let your body relax.

Shake any tension out of your body. Release the tension from your neck and shoulders.

Stand with your hands relaxed by your side.

Bring your attention to your feet.

Imagine roots growing from the bottom of your feet, growing down through the floor, and into the earth, reaching deeper through the layers all the way to the earth's core.

Feel that energy flowing back up through the earth, all around you, up through you, and spilling over you about a foot from the top of your head.

Feel this flowing fountain as it continues to reach down into Mother Earth, pulling up her warm invigorating energy and then lifting it up through you, around you, and over you.

Let this warm sensation flow through you and over you several times until you feel calmer and more centered.

Take a deep breath and say thank you. Continue on with your day, carrying that solid grounded feeling with you.

How did this work for you?

Notice how you felt before you started and then when you finished. How was it?

Think about how you can incorporate this into your daily life and make a few notes here to remind you about the power of this simple technique.

Extra Credit:

You can add color to create a beautiful cycle filled with protection, healing, and love. You can refer to Day 14 for your color symbols and select a color that is ideal for you.

When you visualize the energy flow from Mother Earth in the activity above, imagine that the energy is your chosen color and feel it envelop you with healing, love, and protection that stays with you all this day.

Did you choose a color? Which one? How did this enhance your grounding experience?

Use this space to draw your grounding visualization. Include your roots, Mother Earth, and anything else that spoke to you.

What you've drawn will also pop up in your mind's eye when you're experiencing something and your intuition is knowing a grounding will help. This often happens prior to you even realizing you would benefit. It's like when you put on a raincoat on a sunny day. You don't know why, but you did it. Four hours later you're dry when the unexpected shower pops up! Intuition for the win!

DAY 31

WASH AWAY THE GLOOM

A day to clean up your intuition. Taking conscious action to identify and clean up the things that cloud your sixth sense will really help you raise your vibration, cleanse your energy, and allow clearer intuitive messages.

Creating clear intuition is like washing your mirrors. Removing the dirt, fingerprints, and watermarks enables you to clearly see your gorgeous self. In the same way you wash your mirror, it's time to do an "intuition wash down."

What Kind of Cleaning Do You Need?

Think about what water spots are present on the mirror of your life.

Water spots would be sticky messages of defeat, doubts, or negativity that you take in from social media, news, or conversations.

Fingerprints are like negative things about yourself that you believe or have accepted as truth, but it's time to clear those out, too. Dusty bits can cloud your judgement and eat away at your confidence.

Just imagine the layers of dirt that can pile up on you, brought in by people dumping their bad energy on you every time you see them. Sketch out what this gunk and grime looks like to you and resolve to clear up this mess.

The next page shows you how to start!

Wash Away Negativity in Your Life

Now, it's your turn to take action. You're going to love this part!

Wash a mirror in your life of all its spots.

1) Prepare a spray bottle with white vinegar and water.

2) Spray and wipe the actual mirror, and as you do, visualize all of the negativity washing away from your thoughts.

3) As you do this, visualize letting go of things from your past and present that left an imprint on you.

4) See your worries about the future washing away.

5) Time to let it all go!

As you clean the mirror in your real life, affirm the new, cleaner feeling you have inside:

"I am clear and confident. I see things clearly and I am able to wash away all that is not in harmony with my well-being."

DAY 32

PUTTING A FEATHER IN YOUR CAP

Day 32 is a feather day that brings fun! Think about how feathers appear in your life and how they connect you to your angel. Watch for the many ways feathers show up for you.

Can you think of a more wonderful image than *angel wings?* It's one of my favorites and I'm reminded of it so many times!

You can be, too — just keep your eyes open for a feather. It can appear as a real bird's feather or an image of a feather that you see in your travels in any way, shape, or form.

Quite often, an angel will leave a feather for you to notice that they're nearby.

Color in the feather below while expressing gratitude for all of the times feathers have been placed on your path. Select a color that speaks to you and as you take the action of coloring this image, you dial into angel wings and angels in your even more clearly!

Use this page to tape any additional feathers you find.

These are not just feathers? More like mini cheerleaders! These floaty symbols of hope and freedom can instantly sprinkle a bit of "you've got this" on any gloomy day. Think of each feather in your collection as a high-five from the universe. Their diverse patterns and colors aren't just eye candy—they're little victory flags of birds who've soared high and navigated storms. So, next time life ruffles your feathers, take a peek at your collection and remember: if birds can fly high and free, so can you!

DAY 33

CREATING YOUR OWN PENDULUM

Tap into the Universal power grid by creating your own pendulum. You can make it with simple materials and use it whenever you wish to tap into your own inner wisdom.

Pendulums may be a new concept for you or an everyday activity. It might be a game that you played as a child or with friends.

If you're not already a believer, today is your chance to create and learn to use this simple forgotten tool of the Universe for your greatest good whenever you want.

The term *pendulum* was first used around 1643 in Germany, however the process itself has been around for thousands of years. The scientist Zhang Heng of the Han Dynasty used similar pendulum devices for determining earthquakes. Galileo used a pendulum, as well as, Leonardo da Vinci and Sir Isaac Newton.

Later on, Britain used this process for locating bombs and disposing of them safely. French physicians used pendulums for discovering ailments and allergies. This exercise will have you tapping into the same energetic waves that both General Patton and Nobel Prize winner, Charles Richet used, so you are in good company!

You may have heard of "dowsing" for locating water, minerals, caves, and tunnels, and that is like this process. Albert Einstein believed "dowsing tools" connected with the Universe's electromagnetism.

Just like Thomas Edison said about electricity: "I don't know what it is, but it's there, let's use it."

How to Create your Own Pendulum

1) Supplies: scissors, thread, and a paperclip

2) First cut your thread to a 24-inch length. Then double the thread.

3) Now slip the thread through the curve of one end of your paper clip and pull the thread.

4) The paper clip will dangle freely while you hold the two thread ends with your fingers.

Now to use it!

First relax. No overthinking. Dangle the thread from your fingers with the paperclip about six inches above a flat surface.

Start with the pendulum (or paperclip) in a neutral position, not moving.

Aloud ask for an "absolute yes." Hold your hand and fingers steady and watch which direction the paperclip swings. It might be right to left, forward and backward or it might swing in a circle. Make a note of the movement, and that will be your "yes."

Which way did it move?

> [blank response box]

Ask for an "absolute no." Notice the swing movement again. It will be a different movement, so make a note of what that looks like for you.

Which way did it move?

> [blank response box]

Ask a question that would deliver a "maybe" or "uncertain" response and notice the swing movement.

Write down what happened.

> [blank response box]

Now you will have three distinct directions and three answers that are yours! Each person who tries this may get a different directional swing. That's OK. Even if you do this tomorrow, the swings may be different so test the yes/no/maybe direction at the beginning of each time. Say thank you each time a swing is confirmed.

Make notes here as to what your three directions are and what they mean, or mark them on the chart below.

Practice with seven yes/no questions. Relax each time you ask a question and make a note of the answers.

☐ Yes

☐ No

☐ Maybe or Uncertain

Notice any physical sensations and any intuitive senses you get as you practice with this tool.

Write down your observations here. (For example, hand heavy, arm tingles, felt an answer in my gut, and it was confirmed by the swing).

You can use your homemade pendulum or buy one that you like when you have the chance.

As long as you ask a yes/no question, the pendulum will give you the answer by tapping into the Universal electrical grid that we all operate within on this earth.

The more you practice, the more comfortable and confident you will become. Many intuitive people love to use their pendulum for guidance, and using it to tap into their Universal wisdom. Enjoy this magical and empowering tool.

DAY 34

"POSITIVE VIBES ONLY" ZONE

*You're going along having a good day and suddenly * **bam** * you're bombarded with negativity. People are cranky. Messages are complaining, belittling, or finding fault. Today's activity helps you stay in the "positive vibes only" zone! You'll practice keeping a positive and protected vibe all day and tuning out whatever gets in your way. Protect yourself and your zone to maintain your highest vibration.*

Positive thoughts boost your vibration, your mood, your manifestation, your awesomeness! Today is a negativity-free zone!

Only positive thoughts!

Only positive talk!

Be positive all day long.

Make a note below of any habits of negativity that might slip in and try to throw off your positive groove.

These could include negative conversations, or self-bashing (*I can't, I'm not talented, that doesn't happen for me ...*) or gossiping with friends or listening to newscasts or social media.

Are other people around you being excessively negative? Tattle right here! How often is this happening and who are the biggest offenders?

Taking Stock of Your Overall Day

What do you feel is the biggest negative influence in your life?

Now that you've noticed, what are you going to do about it?!

Fill in the blanks below and make a plan to send this negativity packing.

I've noticed _____ impacts me negatively

and it seems to be _____(frequency).

From now on, I'm going to _____

_____ . I promise to be

diligent regarding this because "I am worthy."

Bonus Time: Put on Your Protective Suit

When you know you're going into a negative place or that you have to be around negative people, here's a way to keep yourself protected. (This also works when you're entering a completely new place and you're uncertain what you'll find.)

This tool helps you pull in your aura so that your natural energy field doesn't mingle with unwanted negativity and then you just put your protective suit on over top!

Step One is pulling in your aura. Do this by visualizing your own energy bubble surrounding you about six feet. Tightly pull in your bubble as snug as you desire. Stand straight with your arms above your head, palms touching. Next, fan your hands away from you, dropping your outstretched arms down to your side. As your arms touch your outer thighs, feel your aura pulling in close.

Step Two is to put on a protective suit. Visualize a pink bubble shield surrounding you so any negativity bounces right off of you. This keeps your joy, love, and positive energy highly charged.

DAY 35

CANDLE FLAME DANCE

Exercise the power of your mind by focusing your energy on the movement of the flame dancing on your candle. As you watch, you can change the level of the flame with just your focus.

In your sacred space or in a quiet spot, light a candle, and relax. Take a couple cleansing breaths as you connect with the flame on your candle.

1) Notice the movement of the flame. Notice the colors dancing within.

2) Intuitively connect with the flame. Notice the swaying of the flame as if you're dancing with it.

3) Now draw your focus to the top of the flame and slowly raise your focus just slightly above the flame.

4) Imagine the flame reaching up to your imaginary line.

5) Encourage the flame to dance higher reaching your focus.

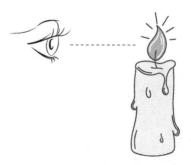

Once the flame has matched your imaginary bar, set a lower bar.

Once your flame has matched that level, boost the flame again by gazing above the tip of the flame.

What happened? Write down as much detail and insight into your candle dancing as you can!

DAY 36

LET YOUR INNER ARTIST COME OUT

You are a creative being at your core. Today is when you let your inner artist out to play. Gather some pencils and colors and see what is waiting to be expressed.

Intuition flows through art. You don't need to be an artist, you just need some colored pencils, crayons or markers. Begin your creative session by asking a sincere question that you'd like insight on.

Then begin drawing and coloring. Use this space to draw your answer.

Relax and take your time. This is not to be rushed. Sincere inspiration and insight will come through. Whatever you ask for, you'll get it!

One of my clients was motivated to get her daughter's paint palette she had used at preschool. She dipped the brush and drew what looked like cherry blossoms. Not an artist, at all, she was so amazed what she created. Afterwards, she had a sense to give her design to a coworker. He began tearing up. He explained he had been missing his mom who had passed. This looked like a painting that had been in her bedroom! Your drawing may be for you or another. Free your spirit from limitations and allow your creativity to just flow. Have faith in the message and draw, paint, or color!

Finding Meaning in Your Art

What did you notice while drawing? Is there a theme in your drawing? Do you see a dominant color? What do you feel is your answer? Write your notes and feelings below, along with the answer you feel showed up for you. (*If you'd like, you can confirm the answer by using your pendulum from Day 33.*)

DAY 37

CREATING YOUR PLAYLIST TO CLARITY

Music is one of the best ways to raise your vibration, so today it's time to crank up some tunes and blast your vibration to the moon and back.

Music moves us, influences our mood, connects us with memories, and affects our overall vibration. Life happens and stressful situations can lower our energy and vibration. If you have a thoughtful musical playlist already prepared, you will have just what is needed whenever those gloomy moments occur.

Start by making a draft list of 15 to 20 songs that have always been favorites of yours. Think about ones from different artists, genres, and different times in your life — this music can be from anywhere!

Play each song and decide if it's uplifting — or maybe it wasn't as high a vibration as you thought. What reaction did you have with each type of music, artist or time frame? What other music or tunes might work even better? Try new things! What about classical, jazz, pop, or folk? See what resonates best with you these days. Make a few notes below on your first impressions.

Now, from the 15 or 20 songs you listened to or thought about, select your 10 most favorite upbeat tunes, the ones that make you smile, feel happy, and in tune with the world, and then put those songs in one place where you can hit play at any time.

Make this your go-to playlist when you feel like you need a boost of good vibes and enhanced peace or clarity.

1) ....

2) ....

3) ....

4) ....

5) ....

6) ....

7) ....

8) ....

9) ....

10) ....

Bonus Time: Pass Along the Musical Magic!

Once you make your list, encourage someone you know to create their own list and help them pull it together. Select a friend, colleague, or family member whom you know is often feeling down or negative, or maybe they are healing from something bad or a recent loss. Your kindness in helping them can be a big boost to them because they will be able to enjoy their own feel-good playlist at the press of a button.

DAY 38

KEEPING THE MUSIC PLAYING

Keep the tunes and fabulous energy flowing on Day 38 by creating a super-charged musical playlist that you can tap into anytime you need your soul charged up.

Today is about charging up your soul with even more musical choices! Maybe there are more that you didn't think about yet, but which would be fun to help you evoke wonderful memories and experiences.

To get you through until you reach the rainbow, add ten more meaningful songs to your ultimate playlist, to create a list that truly inspires, recharges, and uplifts your soul.

Here are nine prompts to get you started on finding those hidden song gems:

1) Think of your favorite memory as a child. Choose a song from that time period. Write that song here:

2) Think of your favorite pet. Choose a song that ties to your animal. Write the song title here:

3) Think of a time when you had a fit of the giggles. Choose a song that matches that memory and write it here:

4) Think of your favorite food dish, one you associate with good times. Even smelling this dish brings a smile to your face and your soul. Choose a song that represents this dish and write it here:

5) What was your super pump-up music you'd play before you'd go out on a date?

Do you have a personal anthem or a major boost kind of song? Write those song titles here:

6) When have you experienced a magical day? Was it at a movie, theme park, wedding, family party or special date? What occurred? What song or songs capture that joy, reminding you of that magical memory?

7) When did you feel overwhelming gratitude, so much so that your heart felt like it was singing? Capture that moment with songs and write them here:

8) Have you experienced a night when stars were twinkling, and you felt all your dreams were coming true? Identify that moment. What songs capture the emotion and memories?

9) What are three of your favorite songs that you just love and that you never go anywhere without?

Now revisit your playlist from Day 37 and incorporate some of the songs you came up with today.

Write out your full playlist and create it using Spotify, Pandora, YouTube or iTunes.

DAY 39

FEELING A FABULOUS WATERFALL

No time to get out in nature? No problem! Consciously create your own cleansing waterfall at home! Feel the surge of power and balance as the water washes down over you.

Shower time can naturally feel so good. Intuitively you sense that your best thinking often happens in the shower. Or maybe you wake up in the shower feeling so refreshed. There is a reason for this!

Showers are natural negative ion generators. The steam and hot water produce the healing benefits of negative ions.

Positive ions sound like they'd be good. *Nope.* They're carbon dioxide molecules without an electron. Positive ions can cause debilitating health, breathing issues, and overall crankiness. Electronics (cell phones, tablets, TVs and computers) and fluorescent lighting increase positive ions. Suddenly you're stressed out, sleepy and cranky.

So, it's negative ions to the rescue! Negative ions increase oxygen flow, boost energy, and help

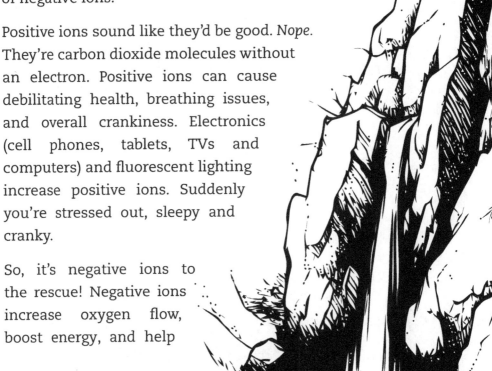

with breathing. The best place for this is good old Mother Nature. In particular, waterfalls are an incredible negative ion resource, with Niagara Falls being one the best places delivering the highest number of negative ions. Beaches, mountains, forests, and oceans supply good amounts too.

But since many of us can't access Niagara Falls every day, we can gain some benefits with our mini waterfall in our bathroom — that's right, your shower!

When you feel sluggish or emotional, you intuitively sense or desire to "clean the air!"! That's the time to turn your shower on. Feel free to get in or just run the water in the shower to allow your room to fill with negative ions.

What did you notice after your last shower? Now that you are aware of this technique, how can you make it work even better for you?

DAY 40

SPRING CLEANING ANY TIME

Take action around your place. Find out how clearing away excess "stuff" that you no longer need makes room for so many more good things and clearer energy to enter your world.

Spring-cleaning was such a fantastic time... said *no one, ever.* Yet, the act of spring-cleaning has a lot of merit! It's a great time for recharging, replenishing, and refreshing.

Even if you recently did clean your place, today choose one room to approach with a good, old-fashioned, spring-cleaning attitude. Wash the sheets and towels. Dust. Wash windows. Sweep every nook and cranny. Wipe down chairs, baseboards, and every corner.

Clean space invites creativity, insight, and clear communication with angels.

Go baby, go!

While cleaning, did you notice if any space seemed to hold specific pockets of dirt or dust?

Did any surprising scents seem to appear while cleaning?

Did any emotions surface? What were you doing at that time?

Why had you postponed cleaning this room? What does it mean to you?

Think about Your Rooms and What They Mean

- Kitchen represents your heart, spirit, and warmth.

- Bedroom represents your connection to life and personal space.

- Bathroom represents releasing and instincts.

- Closet represents hiding.

- Family room represents how you want to project to others.

- Attic represents your mind.

- Basement represents your subconscious.

Did this make sense to you? Now that your area is clean, what message would you like to use to replace your previous feelings about that space?

DAY 41

CONNECTING WITH PEACOCK

Think about your favorite mascot from a sports team or school. That mascot conveys the energy, mood and overall message. Working with Power Animals is the same. They lend their natural energy, instincts and vibration to us. They're like mentors, guiding us.

Peacock has many gifts and messages. Trust your intuition and connect with this power animal!

What messages do you feel Peacock would be giving?

A peacock has feathers resembling eyes.

Your intuition, also known as your third eye, is boosted with the energy, wisdom and guidance of Peacock.

Ask Peacock to work with you to increase your intuition.

Begin with a sincere, heartfelt request, saying,

"Dear Peacock: You are wise and knowledgeable.

You stand out with such elegance, beauty, and confidence. You are grounded and also able to fly to new heights. Please help me have similar confidence in accessing, trusting, and using my intuition. Thank you so much."

Prior to coloring in the feather below, answer the following questions.

1) What is your opinion of peacocks?

2) Do you have experience seeing or working with Peacock?

3) Have you heard a peacock call? Try imitating the sound. Intuitively make the sound. Check on the internet to see how close you were to the right sound!

Get Coloring!

Color in this feather. This will be a symbol for the rest of your journey.

When considering a question and needing insight, ask Peacock to offer confirmation.

You'll see, hear or notice Peacock, which might come to you as a mention, an appearance in your day, or you might mentally see Peacock in your mind's eye.

Be open to the insight and answers of this beautiful bird.

DAY 42

SWEET TIPS FOR SLEEPING SOUNDLY

Getting a restful night of sleep is so important, especially if you want to be your intuitive tip-top self at all times.

Sleep is important. Being well rested boosts your energy level and your intuitive voice. Be sure you're getting quality sleep.

The activities here will help you put your head in a better place tonight so that your rest will be peaceful, refreshing, and uplifting.

Begin by writing 3 things you're grateful for and why. Feel the gratitude deep in your heart for these blessings.

1) ....

2) ....

3) ....

Write three examples of when you heard your intuition today.

1) ....

2) ....

3) ....

Congratulate yourself! Yay!!!!

Now write a little story about one of your favorite moments today. What made it special?

Picture Yourself in Living Color!

Create a colorful image of yourself or your inner self, your favorite angel, animal, or whatever makes you happy. Don't edit yourself — let your creativity flow! Spend some time coloring this picture and making it vibrant and lovely.

Note to Self Before Bedtime:

As your last step in your bedtime routine, snuggle up tight and say to yourself,

"I rock! I am amazing, incredible and marvelous! Woohoo!!! I'm doing great! I have tons to be thankful for and I am so blessed. I deserve a wonderful night's sleep and that is exactly what is coming. I give any cares, worries, and wishes to my team of angels to work on for me overnight and I know that I will awake tomorrow refreshed and ready to take on another day full of fun and intuitive guidance."

DAY 43

TOSSING WHAT'S EXPIRED FROM YOUR LIFE

Today, try clearing out old things in your life that have gone "off." Things that are past their prime and should be trashed. The physical cleansing will make room for newer and brighter things.

Expired and moldy items are bad for your vibration. Go through your refrigerator, pantry, medicine cabinet, and make-up bag and throw away anything that has expired. Ridding yourself and your space from these items removes obstacles. These were just clutter clouding your intuition. In your search for clear intuition, toss what is no longer needed.

Record here what were the three most surprising expiration dates you found! Tell the truth — could be a decade ago but who cares? You're done with it now and this is just to remind you not to keep things forever as you move forward.

1) ....

2) ....

3) ....

Why do you feel you were holding onto these items?

Make a list of the important things you may have to buy fresh or new but for the most part, the things you've just trashed are not needed anyway. It's time to let new things enter your life that have fresh energy!

Things that I need for the pantry, bathroom, cleansers, or make-up bag. Just the essentials!

Bonus Activity – Clear the Decks!

Now — think about other areas of your house, office or your life where you could do a similar clear out of things no longer needed.

What would your new space look like and feel like, once it is clean and clear?

Maybe you can visualize a better place of honor for your sacred space by clearing out some old things that are no longer needed?

Imagine what your clothes closet or linen closet would look like if there was room to breathe — and imagine you opening those doors and finding just what you need quickly and easily with all that excess stuff gone.

DAY

HEDGING AROUND YOUR PERSONAL SPACE

It's time to stretch out and realize you have personal space around you that is valuable and that also needs to stay protected, clear, and vibrant!

Stand with your arms straight out by your side. You'll look like the letter "T."

Notice the area to each side.

With arms still stretched out, now bring your hands to the front of you and notice the area that encompasses.

Stick your arms out behind you. Notice that impressive area. Now above you.

Look at this in a mirror to see just how far your space does reach.

Visualize a protective hedge growing up from the ground and up around you.

No negative influences, vibrations, or people can infiltrate this space. Anyone who comes close to you will feel only kindness from you and you'll feel only kindness from them.

On the next page, draw your hedge. Here's mine to get you thinking.

Image of You and Your Hedge

Hedging Your Bets on Better Days Ahead!

This personal hedge can be anything you want it to be. It is another layer of protection around you that lets in the good but keeps out negativity that you don't want to have in your space.

When you confidently proceed through life with this invisible hedge around you, you keep outside influences from dragging you down. Your intuition will always be clearer and more accurate when your energy is protected!

DAY

ACTION DAY AGAINST STINKING-THINKING

Time to take a few more action steps to really get rid of your stinking-thinking. Learn and practice five easy action steps to get your mind and your attitude smelling like a rose!

Today is an action day to help you change your daily actions so they jibe with your new vibe.

It's always easy to fall back into old thinking — but when you take *action* your body, mind, and spirit accepts the positive changes even more deeply!

Five Quick Action Steps to Kick Stinking-Thinking to the Curb!

1) Take in some inspirational podcasts or videos online rather than listening to or watching gossip or mindless drivel.

2) Practice your intuition daily so you can watch for anyone who is still stuck in a stinking-thinking mindset and steer clear of them. Wash your hands of them and move on to more positive pursuits!

3) Say thank you often and always — to yourself, to your family, to your angels. Count your blessings all the time and you will feel better.

4) Find yourself a new social activity, something you've always wanted to try, like painting, dancing, playing an instrument, or speaking a new language, and sign up for some classes or sessions. You'll be

among people who are moving forward and enjoying life and it will rub off on you!

5) Get moving — jump, dance, hop or shimmy! You already know that moving works and it's one of the best action steps to get your vibe humming. Don't just sit there *stewing* — get *moving!*

Know that you are a divinely guided child of the Universe, and you are protected, loved, and blessed! Feel this in every cell of your body — it's so true! Feel it tingle from the tips of your toes, up to your nose, and all the way to the top of your head.

CONGRATULATIONS!

WOOHOO!!! Congratulations on completing 45 days of boosting your intuition!!!

At this point, you should feel more confident in your abilities to hear and trust your intuitive voice.

Keep practicing! Don't stop. You've built a strong muscle so keep working it!

The more you practice, the stronger you'll become in trusting and taking action on your instincts.

Life will happen. And you'll begin to doubt. When that happens, revisit your favorite days, or just open to the book (trusting your instincts to guide you).

Commit to this process.

At the beginning, you clarified why this was important. You set the intention to know, trust and take action with your intuition. Keep that commitment to yourself.

- Set a daily reminder to celebrate an intuitive message.

- Continue to dive deeper into some of the exercises.

- Practice with a family member or friend.

By continuing to develop and grow your intuition, you'll find other areas growing too: peace, tranquility, love, abundance and being at the right place at the right time!! It's like a magic gift that keeps giving!!!

Trust yourself.

This is your birthright. This is your soul's guidance.

Celebrate your gifts!!!

I'm celebrating YOU, and you should too!!!

Ready to dive deeper into your intuition confidence?

Explore **Intuition Unleashed!**

The course that provides crystal clear clarity so you feel confident in every decision, every single time!

www.intuitionunleashed.com

ABOUT THE AUTHOR

Trish Mckinnley has tremendous intuitive talents that she shares with the world every day. From her offices and within workshops across the world, she works as an intuitive reader, spiritual teacher, and executive coach. She is also an author, speaker, certified crystal healer, and Reiki Master.

Her approach is simple and powerful: she introduces people to proven tools, techniques, and universal wisdom that are completely transforming lives.

Stay connected on social media and visit Trish online to check out her other books and courses!

www.TrishMckinnley.com

Made in the USA
Middletown, DE
06 September 2024

60447615R00097